Better Days & Better Ways

TGT—Trust Gods Timing

Terri Grant

To order additional copies of this book, contact:
Xlibris
1-888-795-4274
www.Xlibris.com
Orders@Xlibris.com

Better Days & Better Ways

TGT- Trust Gods Timing

Publishing Author: Terri T. Grant

Inspiring Authors:
The Late Maya Angelou, (R.I.P)
Miss Cigi Paige, & Miss Rose Williamson

Date: 12/16/18

INTRODUCTION

1. Title: Better Days & Better Ways
    Subtitle: TGT- Trust Gods Timing

2. Author: Terri T. Grant

3. Type: Inspiration and uplifting Poetry

4. Author's Purpose: To inspire and uplift others who may face many struggle, issues, or situations and can't find the right words to encourage themselves or pick themselves back up after a certain level of painful experiences through their life long journey.

FINDING A BETTER WAY, PRAYING FOR BETTER DAYS

There's got to be a better way

I want to see some brighter days,

Just hold on to your faith

Let God show you the way.

Don't give up on your race

One day you'll see his face

Just stay on your paper chase

And watch God replace.

He has you in this quiet place

To shower you with his grace

So let nothing come in between that space.

KEEP PUSHING FORWARD

When its seems like you can't get the pen to the paper and write

because all you have is tears in your eyes

And you don't think you can continue the fight,

Just push through it with all your might

and let God show you his guiding light.

Please know it's going to be alright

Dry your eyes and don't worry.

Pray each day and night

and give God all the Glory!

You are gonna make it through this race

Hold your head up, and fix your face.

God will give you tender mercy,

and save you by his amazing grace.

WHERE DID I GO WRONG?

Where did I go wrong and did not listen?

I guess this is all apart of God's mission.

I'm alive and thankful for this day.

Lord God, I ask that you continue making a way.

 Lord I am tired of being blind,

Please help me organize these thoughts running through my mind.

When will it be my time to shine?

Wait my child, wait patiently

In due time you will see

All that I have planned for you to be.

Just keep your faith strong and repeat after me.

"I come to give you life more abundantly",

"Resist the devil and he will flee"!

Also remind yourself constantly,

that you serve a God who is high & mighty!

RISE ABOVE IT ALL

Why am I afraid to live?

When this world is filled with such amazing things.

Still, I'm just so afraid to live my dreams.

For I have seen the many things

That life can often bring,

Still I'm afraid to live my dreams!

I am afraid my father to do it alone,

but I know I have to keep pushing on.

Lord keep me humble, and keep me strong,

Father God I know it won't be long.

I want success, I want it all,

Even if I stumble, even if I fall

Raise me up to conquer it all.

It's time to rise, and

stop focusing on the fall just tell yourself.

I'm gonna rise above it all!

ONE STEP AT A TIME

I'm learning to take things one step at a time

sooner or later success will be mine!

If I can stop my racing and wandering mind,

I know for a fact that I will be fine,

God answer prayers right on time.

I have to remind myself to take things one step at a time.

I know what I want and that's an importance to success,

Just sit back and wait and watch God bless!

God gives us all test

Just to see if we can make it through any mess

so do your best, and God will handle the rest

Keep your mind focused on God

and remind yourself to take things one step at a time.

BETTER DAYS

I want to see better and brighter days

Lord, build me up to be great and better by the way.

Father please hear these things I say!

I need you more and more each day.

Lead me in the the paths of righteousness for your name sake!

In jesus precious name I pray.

Make me humble and make me whole

Lord save my little old noble soul.

I want everything back that the devil stole.

God let him know he has no control.

Thank you father for making me bold!

Father God purify my soul.

This world God is just so cold.

I want to fulfill all of my goals

Lord have mercy on my soul.

Acrostic Poem

T- Tremendous

E- Excellent

R- Relentless

R- Radiant

I- Intelligent

Try to create a Acrostic poem using your name.

I Made It Through

Hey, Hey what can I say

I made it through this dark gloomy day.

In spite all the negativity that came my way.

I still managed to find a way

To bow my head and began to pray.

I really wanted to be left alone today

especially after all of the disturbing news that came my way.

God said, "no, no my child, not today!

Where there is a will, there is a way.

Don't get your spirit all down today.

Tomorrow, you can look forward to a better and brighter day!

I've already prepared the way!

Just follow my steps, and you'll be ok!

Prayer Poem to God

Thank you Lord for your love, advice, and guidance

Also your love, and kindness.

You are my helper, and my keeper

Such an awesome an amazing teacher

You are forever watching over me

I can't help but give you glory!

You are true, and I love you God!

I want a more joyful and happy life

With no sadness or sorrow

I am tired of having to beg and borrow

God please show me a better tomorrow!

GOD LOVES YOU!

THIS LITTLE BIG HEART OF MINE

This little big heart of mine

If only you knew of the many nights I cried

all the painful experiences from my past,

I kept all bottled up on the inside.

There were many days and nights I wished I had died

I felt as if no one could ever understand the tears that I cried.

Until one day God came and stood by my side and

told me everything was gonna be alright,

I saw every teardrop that fell from your eyes.

Now you have to let the past go because

the battle is not your, its mine!

You Can Fly

Fly high like the birds in the sky

Fly high and take the world by surprise

Fly high, Conquer, Rise, and Strive

Fly high, during the day and night!

Fly high lil birdie,

Now is your time!

CANCER YOU'RE A LIE

In 2018 Cancer wanted to steal my life

But God said, "No"!

We're not going out without putting up a fight

So dry your eyes, and stop worrying

Remember weeping may endure for a night

But joy comes in the morning light. (Psalms) 30:5

FLY HIGH

You are like the Eagle in the sky

Soar high,

You are like a Lion in its den

Give a deep roar from within

You are as beautiful as a Dove

Thank God up above

So fly high my little lightning Bug!

ACROSTIC POEM

Using my Child's name

T- Terrific

E- Extravagant

R- Remarkable

R- Realist

I- Intelligent

O- Outstanding

N- Nice

If you have children, try creating one using your child's name!

ACROSTIC POEM

*Try This: Use full sentences to create a poem with your name.

T- is for thoughtful, always thinking of others.

E- is for Emotional, intense feelings whether crying or laughter.

R- is for Remarkable, joyful and fun to be around.

R-is for Relaxing, you put people at ease.

I- is for intelligent, you have a brilliant mind to do whatever!

G- is for Generous, a kind heart and loving spirit.

R- is for Reflective, always in deep thought

A- is for Artistic, full of creative ideas and beautiful voice.

N- is for Nice, a very sweet soul.

T- is for Tenacious, never gives up and don't you ever give up, God's Child

Best Life

Live your best life

Conquer, Rise, and Strive!

Forget about all those dark

memories from your past,

that you have hidden on the inside

just ask God for his mighty strength,

and his Holy Spirit to abide.

So by all means,

Live your best life!

BEAUTY WITHIN

You have beauty within, your beauty can mend.
Your beauty within, shines bright through your skin,
Your beauty is outstanding, and it sets a trend
with you is where beauty begins.
So let your beauty shine bright my friend!

TRUST GODS TIMING

Trust Gods timing, It's always right!

He will guide you through the day and night.

He will hold and protect you.

Love and never reject you,

he won't allow any weapons to ever form against you,

So trust Gods Timing and believe that his every word is

true!

Printed in the United States
By Bookmasters